A Keepsake

MARYLAND'S EASTERN SHORE

Antelo Devereux Jr.

SCHIFFER PUBLISHING

4880 Lower Valley Road · Atglen, PA 19310

Bohemia River

INTRODUCTION

There is something peaceful and serene about the Eastern Shore of the Chesapeake Bay. Its low-lying, flat farmland with estuarial marsh edges is penetrated and drained by numerous river systems. First occupied by Native Americans and then colonized by the English led by Captain John Smith of the Virginia Company, this portion of Maryland has been fertile ground for farming and fishing for generations.

The region lies south of the busy I-95 metropolitan corridor and has about it a slightly genteel southern flavor. While farming remains strong, the hunting and fishing economies are suffering—once-abundant wildfowl, fish, crab, and oyster takes have slowly diminished because of overfishing combined with the bay's pollution with silt and fertilizer runoff from the many watersheds that feed it. Additionally, sea level rise threatens the very existence of fishing villages along the marshes and places, such as Smith Island, which are barely above sea level.

Over time the region has become a destination for vacationers and boaters from along the metropolitan corridor. No doubt they are attracted to, enjoy, and value the natural resource that the Eastern Shore represents. Today, organizations such as the Chesapeake Bay Foundation and Riverkeepers play an active role in reversing the destructive trends that have impaired the viability of the bay and the local economies so dependent on it.

I hope my photographs will entertain viewers and, more importantly, remind them of the valuable and irreplaceable asset the Chesapeake Bay and its environs represents.

Chesapeake City

Chesapeake City

Tolchester

Kennedyville

Wild turkey

Snow geese

Oystershells

Georgetown, Sassafras River

St. Francis Xavier Church, Warwick

Mount Harmon

Magnolia flower

Betterton

Chestertown, Chester River

Chester River

Chestertown

Chestertown

Saint Paul's Pilgrim Holiness Church, Oxford

Oxford

Kent Island

Chestertown

Kent Island Narrows

Eastern Neck Island

Kent Island Narrows

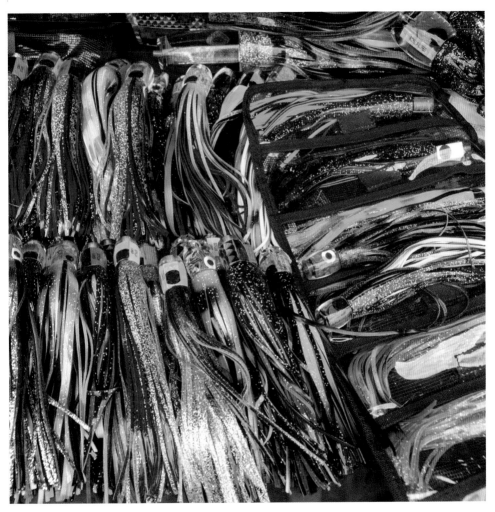

Stevensville

Smith Island crab skiffs, Chester River

Skipjack, Chester River

Washington College, Chestertown

Centreville

Chestertown

Old Wye Episcopal Church, Wye Mills

BAY DREDGING LICENSE

22

DEPT. OF CHESAPEAKE BAY AFFAIRS

10 ADULT
LIFEJACKETS

Chestertown

Chesapeake Bay Maritime Museum, St. Michaels, Miles River

Oyster shucking

The Chesapeake Bay was once one of the greatest oyster producing places on earth. Dozens of Baltimore companies shipped fresh shucked oysters in tins like these, packed in ice, to big city restaurants in the northeast as well as markets in the Midwest and American West. How many of these can you find that used images of oysters to entice the buyer?

Chesapeake Bay Maritime Museum, St. Michaels, Miles River

Tilghman Island

Tilghman Island

St. John's Chapel, Tilghman Island

Tilghman Island

Deal Island

Tilghman Island

Knapp's Narrows

Wye Mills

Easton

Easton

Oxford, Tred Avon River

Oxford, Tred Avon River

St. Michaels, Miles River

Chesapeake Bay Maritime Museum, St. Michaels, Miles River

Cambridge

Cambridge

Christ Episcopal Church, Cambridge

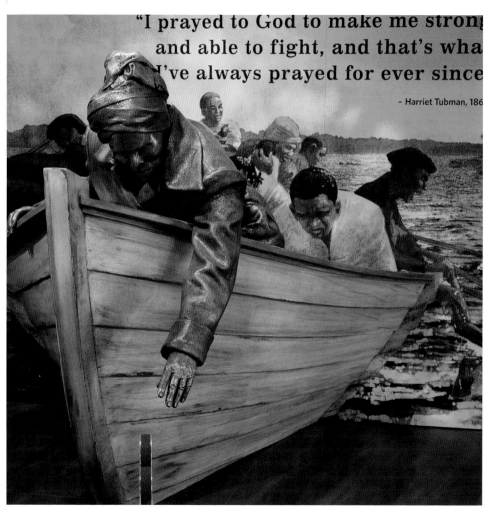

"I prayed to God to make me strong and able to fight, and that's what I've always prayed for ever since

- Harriet Tubman, 186

Harriet Tubman National Historical Park

Hoopers Island

Cambridge

Wingate, Honga River

Choptank, Choptank River

Blackwater National Wildlife Refuge

Old Trinity Church, Church Creek

Queen Anne's County Courthouse, Centreville

Hoopers Island

Blackwater National Wildlife Refuge

Quail hunting

Ward Museum of Wildfowl Art, Salisbury

Egret

Along Bishop's Head Road

Hoopers Island

Fishing Creek

Bald eagles, Blackwater National Wildlife Refuge

Wingate, Honga River

Great blue heron, Blackwater National Wildlife Refuge

Ospreys, Blackwater National Wildlife Refuge

Blackwater National Wildlife Refuge

Wye Mills

Snow Hill

Snow Hill

Pocomoke City, Pocomoke River

Salisbury, Wicomico River

Crabbing

Elliott Island

Rockawalkin, Wicomico River

Whitehaven, Wicomico River

BUILT 1744
IN THE REIGN OF KING GEORGE II

11784

Princess Anne

St. John's United Methodist Church, Deal Island

Rumbly

Smith Island

Smith Island

Crisfield

Rumbly

Chesapeake Bay

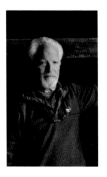

Antelo Devereux Jr. has been making photographs since he was given a Kodak Duaflex II box camera at age 10. Thus began a hobby that has grown increasingly serious as time has gone by. He is a graduate of Harvard University and has taken several courses at the Maine Media Center; exhibited in Maine, Vermont, Pennsylvania, and Delaware; and published 10 photography books. He spends his time in Pennsylvania and Maine with his family.

Other Schiffer Books by the Author:
Coastal Maine, ISBN 978-0-7643-5575-2
Brandywine Valley, ISBN 978-0-7643-5574-5
The Jersey Shore, ISBN 978-0-7643-5576-9

Other Schiffer Books on Related Subjects:
Chesapeake Wildlife: Stories of Survival and Loss, Pat Vojtech, ISBN 978-0-8703-3536-5
Bodine's Chesapeake Bay Country, A. Aubrey Bodine and Jennifer Bodine, ISBN 978-0-8703-3562-4

Copyright © 2022 by Antelo Devereux Jr.

Library of Congress Control Number: 2021942840

Designed by Chris Bower
Type set in Bell MT/Cambria

ISBN: 978-0-7643-6364-1
Printed in India

Published by Schiffer Publishing, Ltd.
4880 Lower Valley Road
Atglen, PA 19310
Phone: (610) 593-1777; Fax: (610) 593-2002
Email: Info@schifferbooks.com
Web: www.schifferbooks.com

For our complete selection of fine books on this and related subjects, please visit our website at www.schifferbooks.com. You may also write for a free catalog.

Schiffer Publishing's titles are available at special discounts for bulk purchases for sales promotions or premiums. Special editions, including personalized covers, corporate imprints, and excerpts, can be created in large quantities for special needs. For more information, contact the publisher.

We are always looking for people to write books on new and related subjects. If you have an idea for a book, please contact us at proposals@schifferbooks.com.